David, we're PREGNANT!

David, we're PREGNANT!

101 Cartoons for
Expecting Parents
by Lynn Johnston

 **Meadowbrook Press**

Distributed by Simon & Schuster

New York

Library of Congress Catalog Number: 77-82214

Publisher's ISBN: 0-88166-184-8
Simon & Schuster Ordering Number: 0-671-76018-1

Published by Meadowbrook Press, 18318 Minnetonka Boulevard,
Deephaven, MN 55391.

BOOK TRADE DISTRIBUTION by Simon & Schuster, a division of
Simon and Schuster, Inc., 1230 Avenue of the Americas, New York, NY 10020.

96 95 94 93 92 91 6 5 4 3 2 1

Printed in the United States of America

Introduction

Once upon a time there were no cartoons on the ceiling of my examining room. From my point of view, of course, the examining room was always an interesting place where I met fascinating people, with perplexing problems for me to solve. The relationship was simple and direct. The patients had questions. I had gone to medical school and learned answers. The examining room was the place where the questions and the answers got together. Both patient and doctor went in for the same purpose, and both went out satisfied.

One day a perceptive woman, who had lain all too long on the table counting the dots on an otherwise blank ceiling, asked me why I didn't put any pictures up there. I didn't have a good answer, but I realized it was a good question. And I was struck with the realization that the patient's point of view from the examining table was very different from the doctor's point of view. A host of new questions started to crowd in.

When does pregnancy really begin? Is it, like we were taught in school, at the precise moment when sperm and egg join together, or is it earlier, when a couple start to plan and yearn for a family? Or is it perhaps later, with the realization of pregnancy, and the growing awareness of the life within?

What is pregnancy? Is it the weight gains and the blood pressures and the morning sicknesses and the strange symptoms the doctor sees? Or is it the hopes and fears, and joys and tremblings, and a new body to adjust to, and a new shape to learn to love? Is it a time for parents to prepare for their new exciting role to come?

What are prenatal classes? A passing fad to keep patients occupied? Or an opportunity for us to learn about our bodies and ourselves, to learn the skills needed for the awesome task ahead?

What is labor? Is it a series of uterine contractions working to dilate the cervix and expel a new baby into the world? Or is it a dreaded yet anticipated experience, unknown and unknowable, through which one must pass with only old wives' tales and untested prenatal classes as uncertain guides?

Indeed, what is the new baby? A little patient to be weighed and tested, and formulas to be adjusted? Or a new individual who will change lovers into parents, and mates into a family, with new joys and sleepless nights?

There are many books about pregnancy, but most are written from the professional's point of view. The patient's answers to these questions are rarely expressed. In this book, Lynn has given the parents' viewpoint, clearly and pointedly. For parents, for parents-to-be, and for professionals too.

And now I have cartoons on my ceiling.

MURRAY W. ENKIN, M.D.

9

Don't be so depressed.... Remember when getting your period was a good sign ?
LYNN

15

I'm pretty sure that I am....
but what if I'm not.... what if
it's negative... or nerves... or
imagination. Actually, I'm
positive I am. I'll phone
for a checkup. But what
if they tell me I'm not....
better wait another week
to make sure..... No. Why
wait if I'm POSITIVE!...
Then again... what if I'm not....
On the other hand...
maybe.........

Lynn

22

23

25

I don't understand it, Dad... Jan just found out she's pregnant—but I'm the one with the knots in my stomach!
LYNN

Well, congratulations, Elly!..... You know, Lewis & I would have had children...but, we just don't have the patience.
LYNN

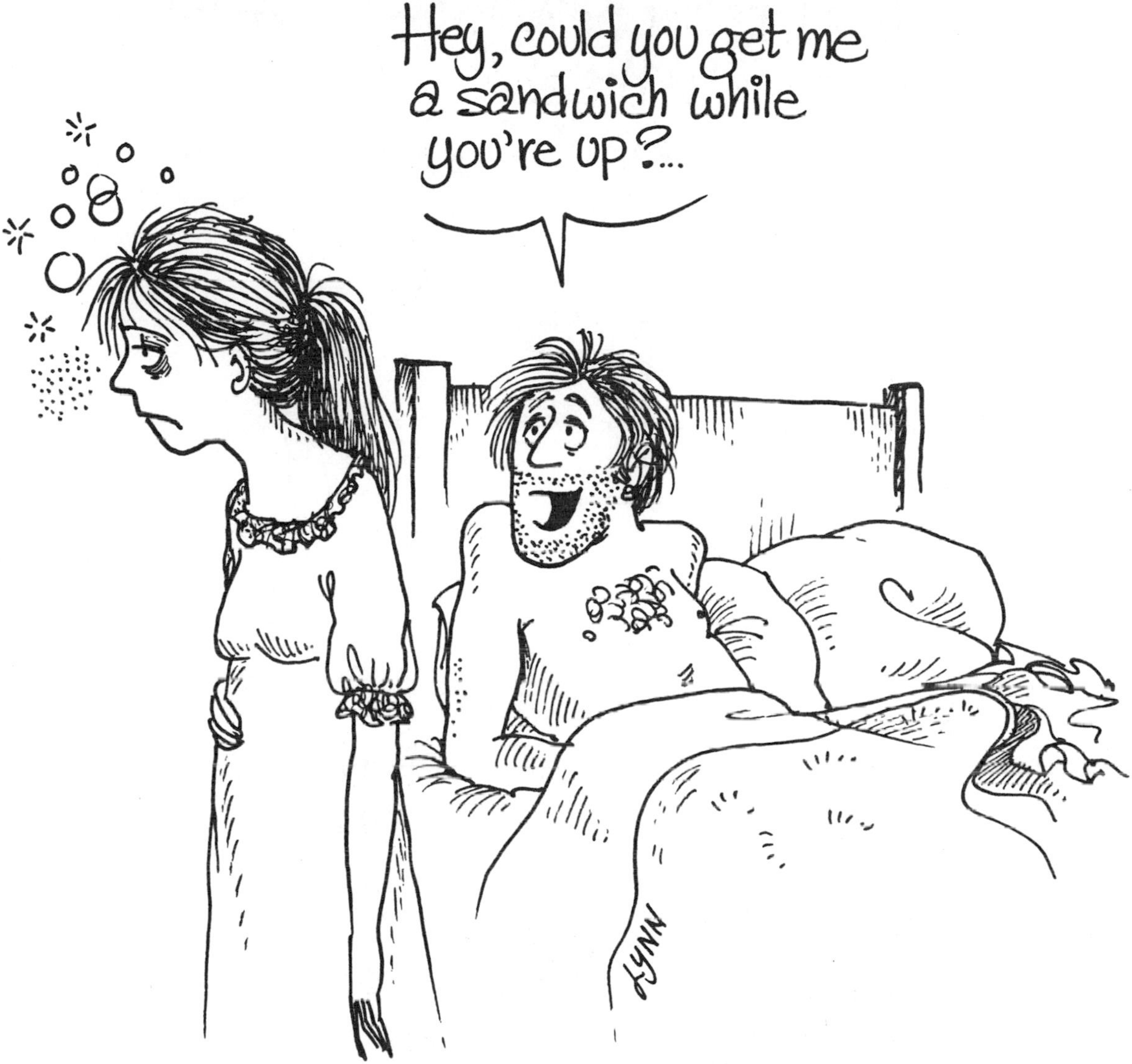
Hey, could you get me a sandwich while you're up?...
LYNN

41

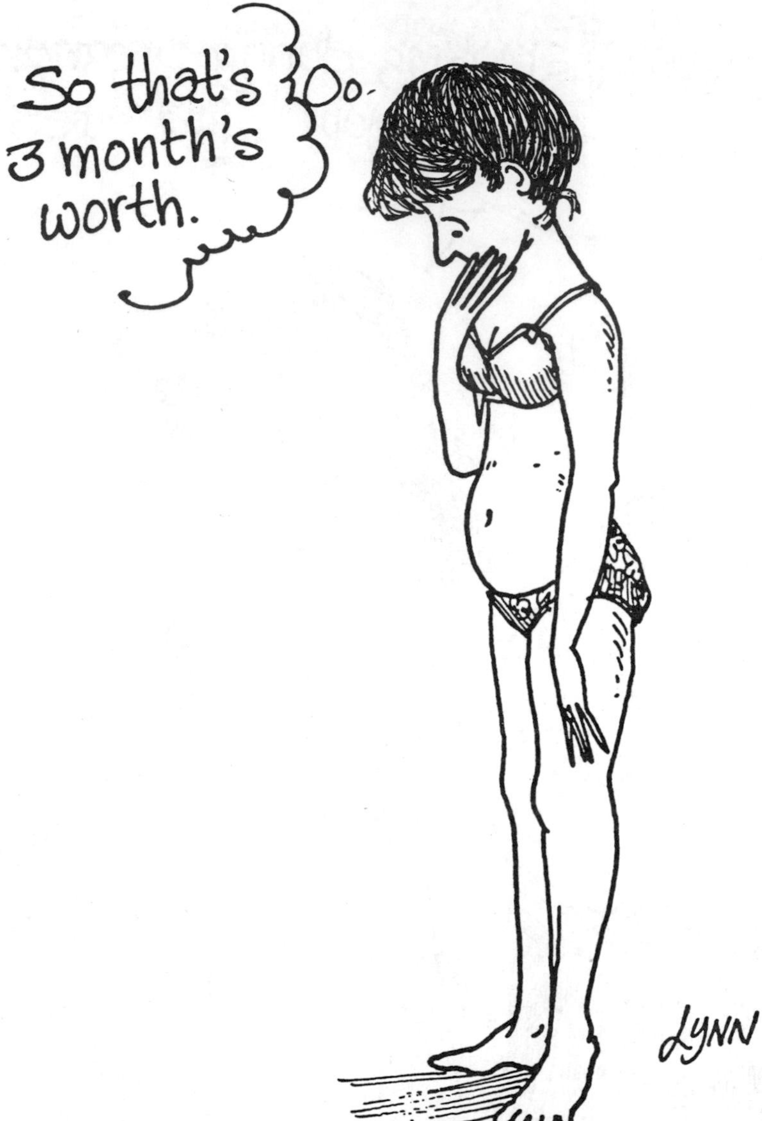
So that's 3 month's worth.
LYNN

46

In seven months, you'll be carting around a kid this big!
TURKEY 7 LBS.
FRESH POULTRY
LYNN

49

51

54

Mom, Ken's agreed to go to prenatal classes with Barbie....

Lynn

58

60

And I wish you'd stop saying "KNOCKED UP"!

Jynn

61

63

Now, I want you to imagine your vagina is an elevator. Lift it up... UP... UP...
LYNN

Mother's coming to give you the benefit of her experience....
LYNN

While you're waddling around town - could you pick me up a copy of the evening edition?

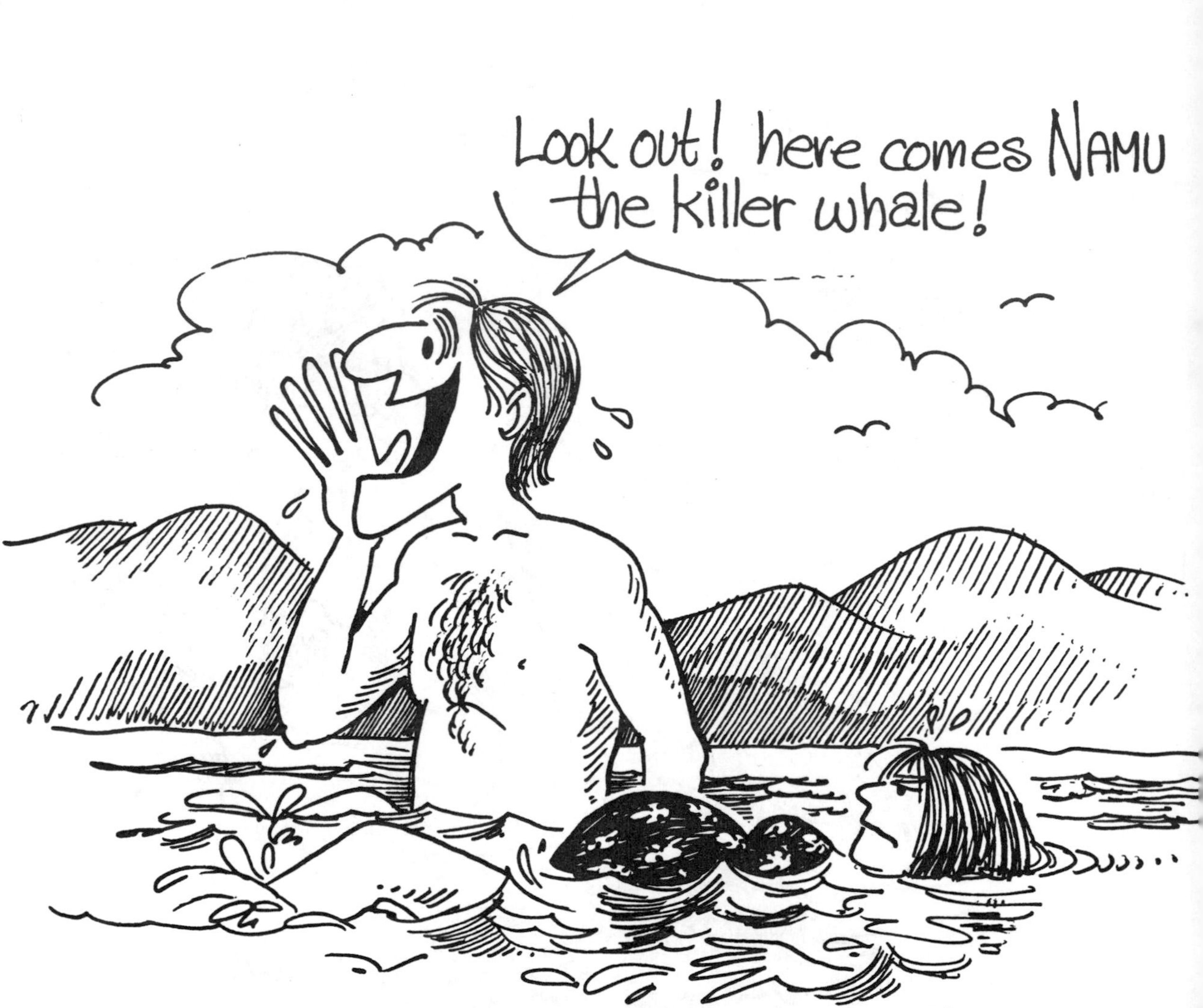
Look out! here comes NAMU the killer whale!
LYNN

No matter how I lie, I'm uncomfortable....
I think I'm going to have to learn
how to sleep standing up.

JYNN

76

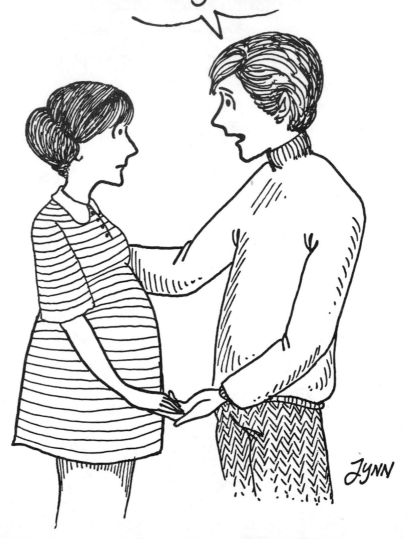

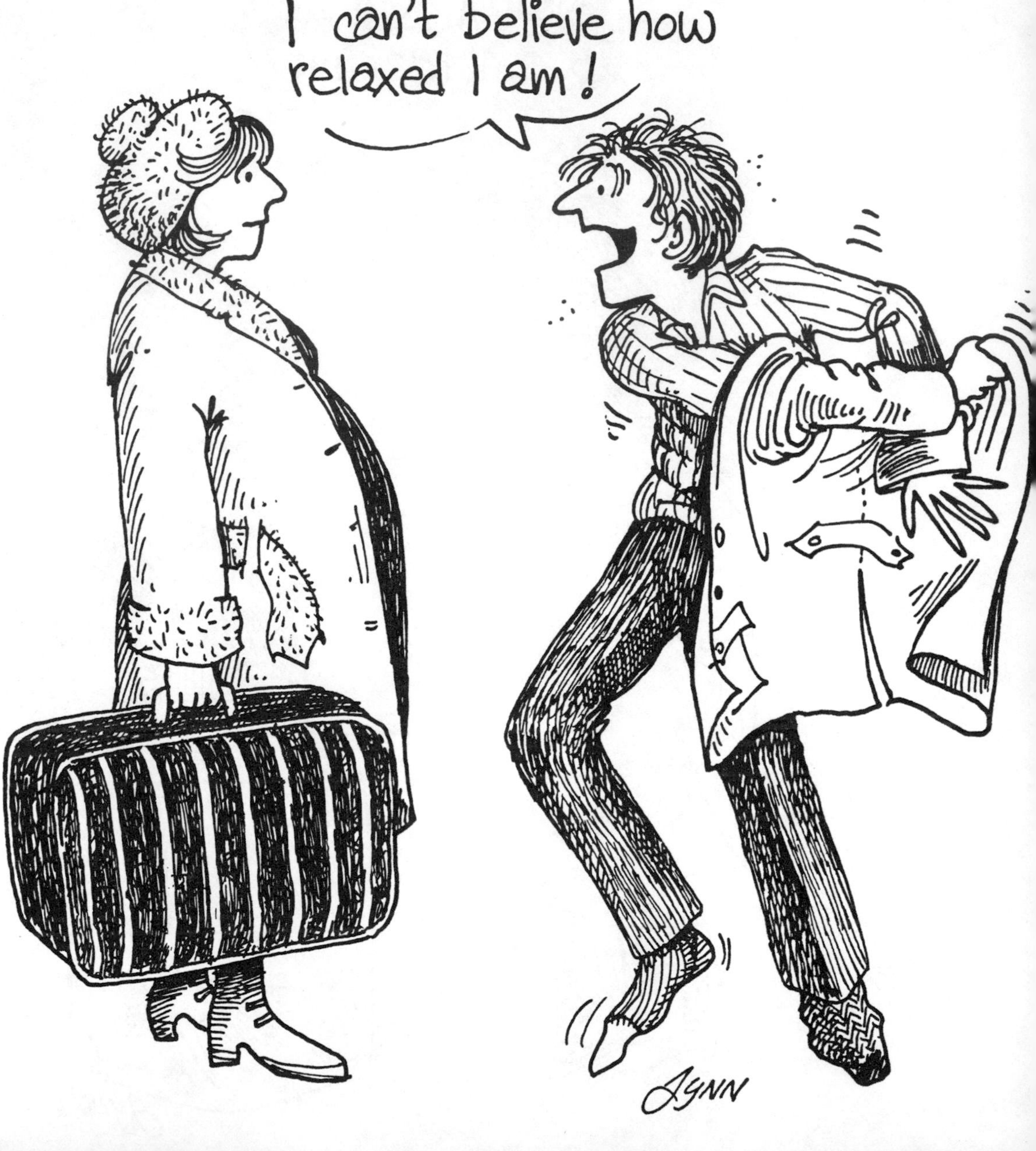
I can't believe how relaxed I am!
LYNN

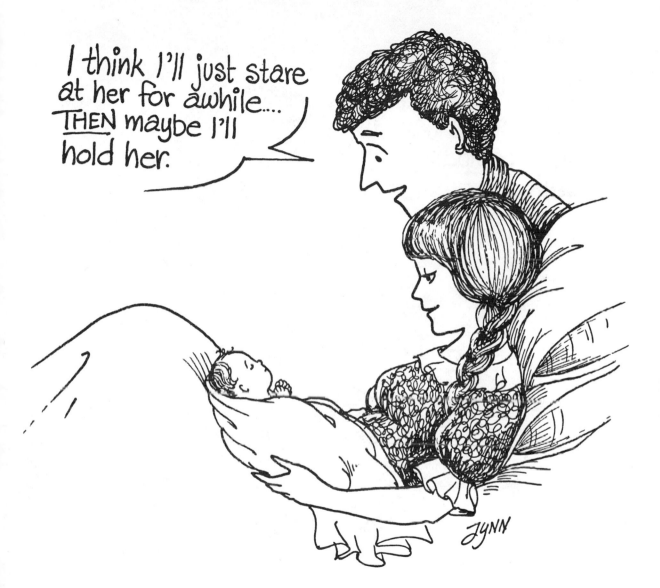

96

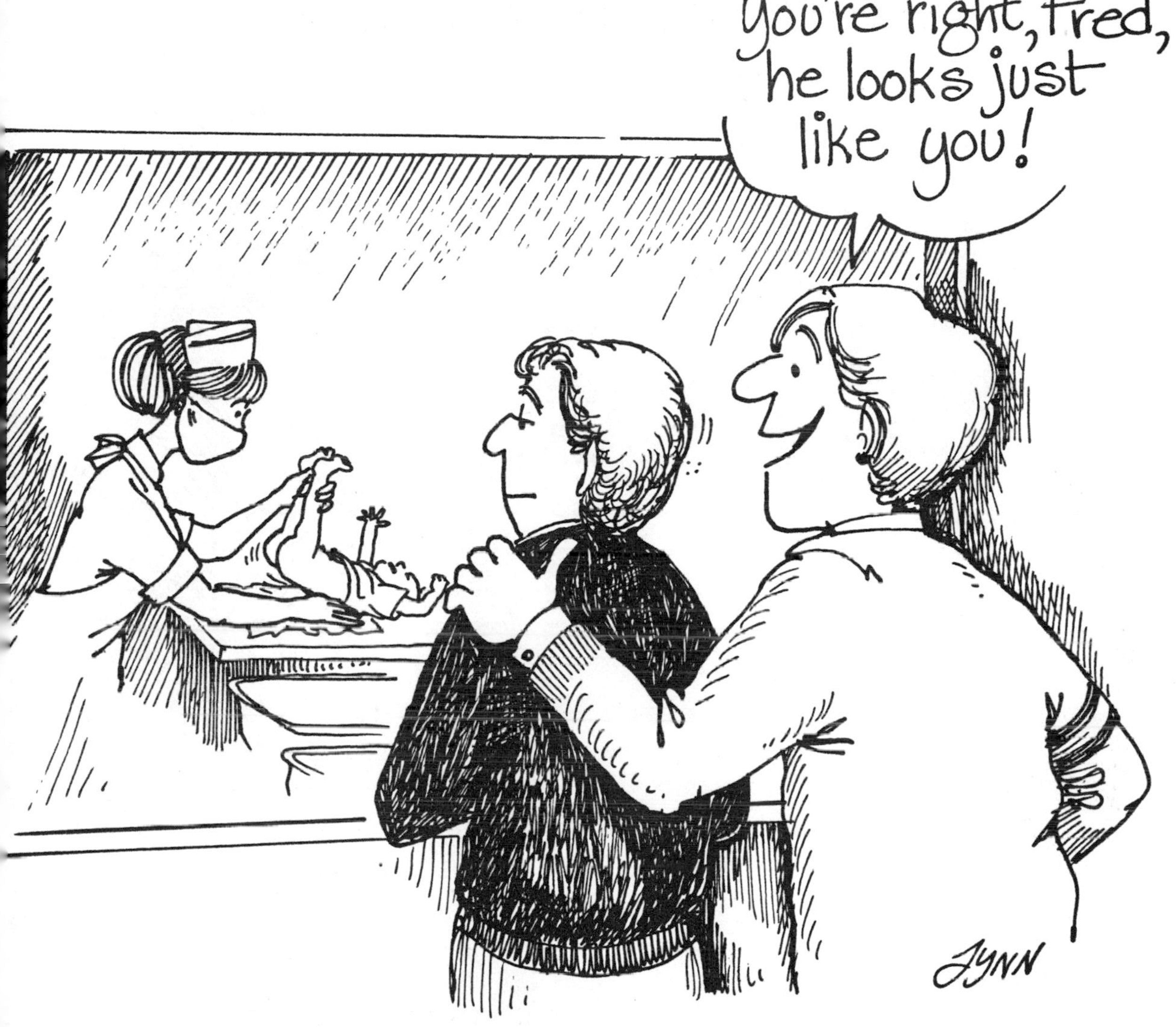
You're right, Fred, he looks just like you!
LYNN

98

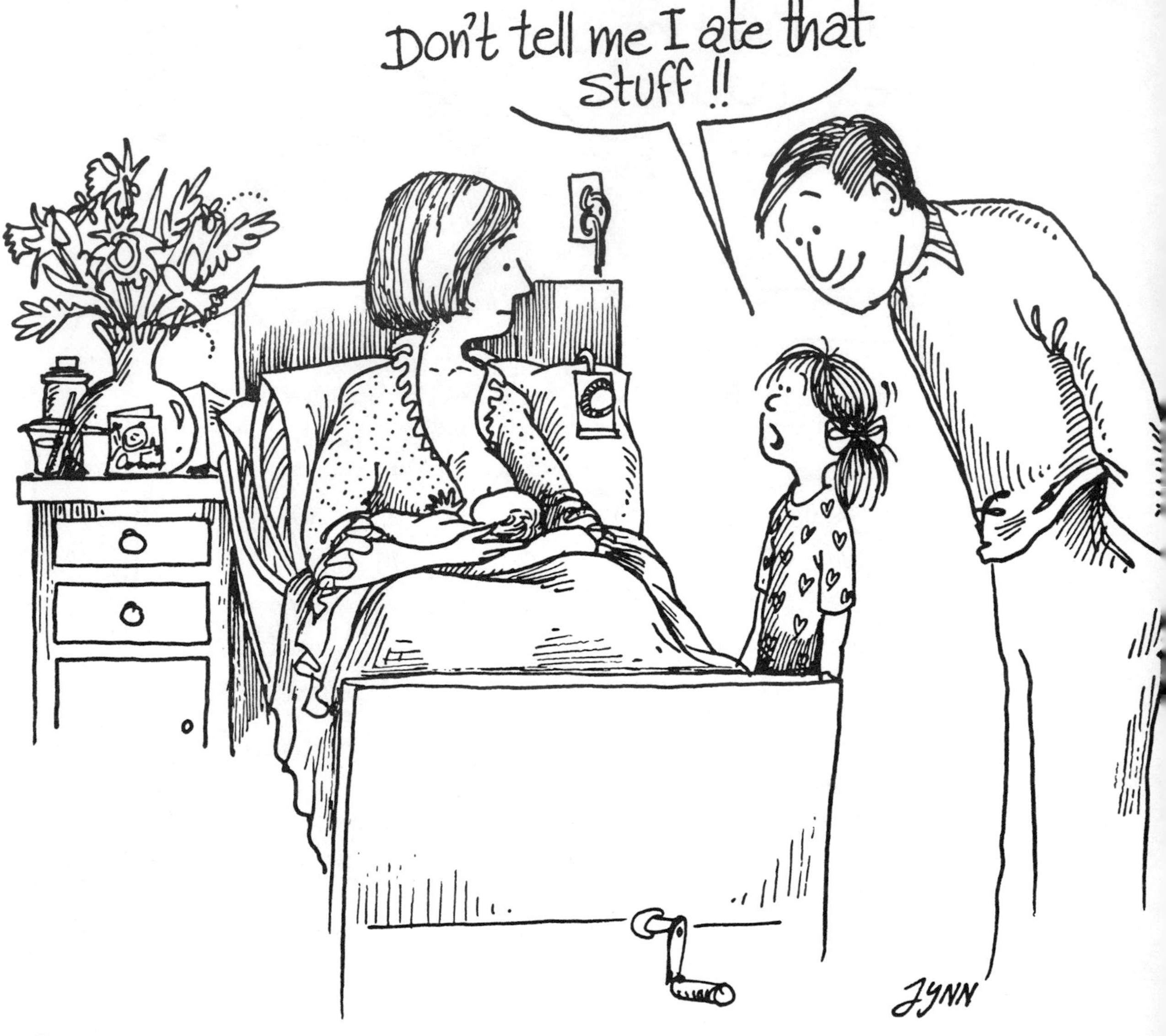
Don't tell me I ate that stuff !!
JYNN

103

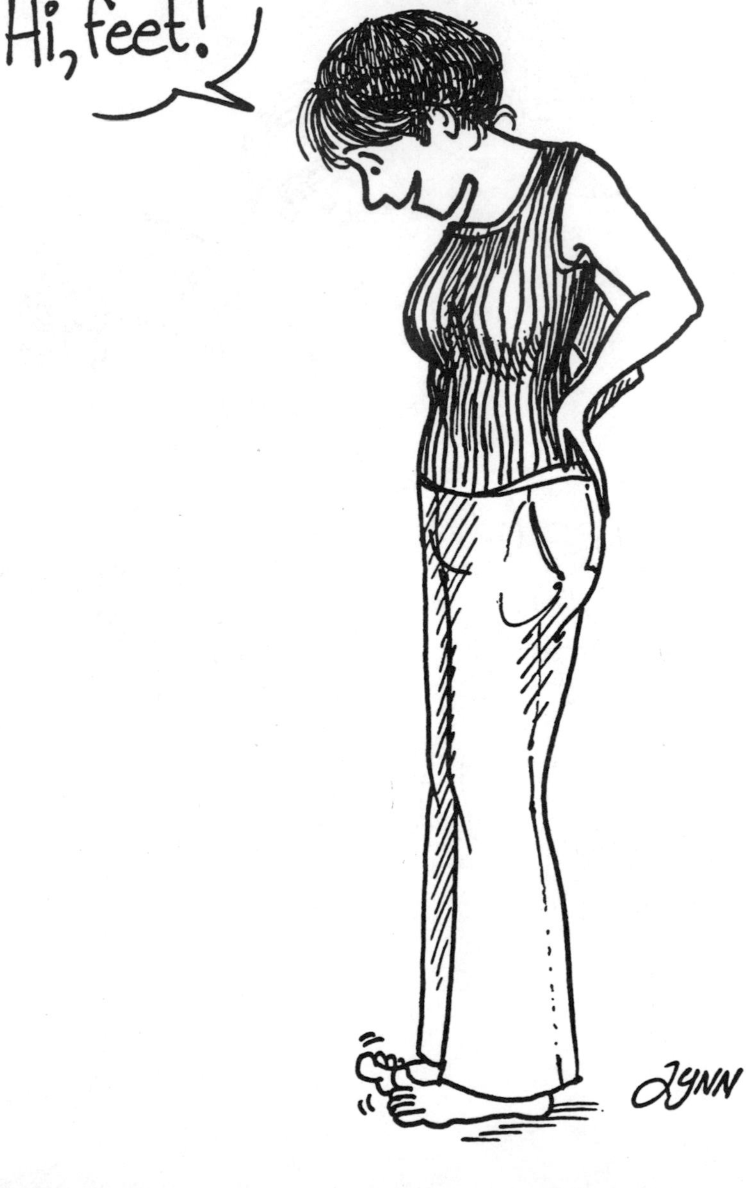
Hi, feet!
LYNN

Meet Lynn Johnston

Lynn Johnston is North America's best-selling female cartoonist. She draws much of her material from close observation of her family: Aaron, Katie and husband Rod (a dentist). Lynn's deft, humorous depictions of life with kids have provided her with material for three books published by Meadowbrook Press, plus an internationally syndicated comic strip, *For Better or For Worse*. Lynn and her family live in Corbeil, Ontario.

& Her Books:

DAVID, WE'RE PREGNANT!

101 laughing-out-loud cartoons that accentuate the humorous side of conceiving, expecting, and giving birth. A great baby shower gift, it's the perfect way to bolster the spirits of any expectant couple.

Order # 1049

HI, MOM! HI, DAD!

A side-splitting sequel to *DAVID, WE'RE PREGNANT!* 101 cartoons on the first year of childrearing—all those late night wakings, early morning wakings, and other traumatic "emergencies" too numerous to list.

Order # 1139

DO THEY EVER GROW UP?

This third in her series of cartoon books is a hilarious survival guide for parents of the tantrum and pacifier set, as well as a side-splitting memory book for parents who have lived through it.

Order # 1089

DADS SAY THE DUMBEST THINGS!

by Bruce Lansky & Ken Jones

Lansky and Jones have collected all the greatest lines dads have ever used to get kids to stop fighting in the car, feed the pet, turn off the TV while doing their homework, and get home before curfew from a date. It includes such winners as: "What do you want a pet for—you've got a sister" and "When I said 'feed the goldfish,' I didn't mean feed them to the cat." A fun gift for dad.

Order # 4220

MOMS SAY THE FUNNIEST THINGS!

by Bruce Lansky

Bruce Lansky has collected all the greatest lines moms have ever used to deal with "emergencies" like getting the kids out of bed in the morning, cleaned, dressed, to school, to the dinner table, undressed, and back to bed. It includes such all-time winners as: "Put on clean underwear—you never know when you'll be in an accident" and "If God had wanted you to fool around, He would have written 'Ten Suggestions.'" A fun gift for mom.

Order # 4280

THE BEST BABY NAME BOOK IN THE WHOLE WIDE WORLD

by Bruce Lansky

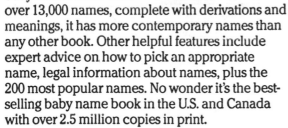

This really is the best baby name book! With over 13,000 names, complete with derivations and meanings, it has more contemporary names than any other book. Other helpful features include expert advice on how to pick an appropriate name, legal information about names, plus the 200 most popular names. No wonder it's the best-selling baby name book in the U.S. and Canada with over 2.5 million copies in print.

Order # 1029

THE BABY NAME PERSONALITY SURVEY

by Bruce Lansky & Barry Sinrod

This fascinating book is based on a national survey of 75,000 parents—the largest name research project ever. It reveals the images and stereotypes associated with 1,400 popular and unusual names. Find out what other people think of the names you're considering before you make a decision that will last a lifetime. A must for every parent-to-be!

Order # 1270

Order Form

Quantity	OTHER BABY CARE BOOKS BY MEADOWBROOK:		Order No.	Unit Cost	Total
	Title	Author			
	10,000 Baby Names	Lansky, Bruce	1210	$3.50	
	Baby Name Personality Survey, The	Lansky/Sinrod	1270	$7.00	
	Baby Talk	Lansky, Bruce	1039	$4.00	
	Best Baby Name Book in Whole Wide World	Lansky, Bruce	1029	$5.00	
	Best Baby Shower Book, The	Cooke, Courtney	1239	$6.00	
	Birth Partner's Handbook, The	Jones, Carl	1309	$6.00	
	Dads Say the Dumbest Things!	Lansky/Jones	4220	$6.00	
	David, We're Pregnant!	Johnston, Lynn	1049	$6.00	
	Do They Ever Grow Up?	Johnston, Lynn	1089	$6.00	
	Feed Me! I'm Yours	Lansky, Vicki	1109	$8.00	
	First-Year Baby Care	Kelly, Paula	1119	$7.00	
	Getting Organized for Your New Baby	Bard, Maureen	1229	$5.00	
	Grandma Knows Best	McBride, Mary	4009	$5.00	
	Hi, Mom! Hi, Dad!	Johnston, Lynn	1139	$6.00	
	Maternal Journal, The	National Parenthood Assn.	3171	$10.00	
	Moms Say the Funniest Things!	Lansky, Bruce	4280	$6.00	
	Mother Murphy's Law	Lansky, Bruce	1149	$4.50	
	Our Baby's First Year Calendar	Meadowbrook Creations	3179	$10.00	
	Parents' Guide to Baby & Child Medical Care	Hart, Terril	1159	$8.00	
	Practical Parenting Tips	Lansky, Vicki	1179	$7.00	
	Pregnancy, Childbirth, and the Newborn	Simkin/Whalley/Keppler	1169	$12.00	
				Subtotal	
			Shipping and Handling (see below)		
			MN residents add 6.5% sales tax		
				Total	

YES! Please send me the books indicated above. Add $1.50 shipping and handling for the first book and 50¢ for each additional book. Add $2.00 to total for books shipped to Canada. Overseas postage will be billed. Allow up to 4 weeks for delivery. Send check or money order payable to Meadowbrook Press. No cash or C.O.D.'s, please. Prices subject to change without notice. **Quantity discounts available upon request.**

Send book(s) to:

Name _____

Address _____

City _____ State _____ Zip _____

Telephone (_____)_____ Purchase order number (if necessary) _____

Payment via:

☐ Check or money order payable to Meadowbrook Press (No cash or C.O.D.'s, please.) Amount enclosed $_____

☐ Visa (for orders over $10.00 only.)   ☐ MasterCard (for orders over $10.00 only.)

Account # _____ Signature _____ Exp. Date _____

A FREE Meadowbrook Press catalog is available upon request.
You can also phone us for orders of $10.00 or more at 1-800-338-2232.

Mail to:
Meadowbrook, Inc.
18318 Minnetonka Boulevard, Deephaven, Minnesota 55391

(612) 473-5400   Toll-Free 1-800-338-2232   Fax (612) 475-0736